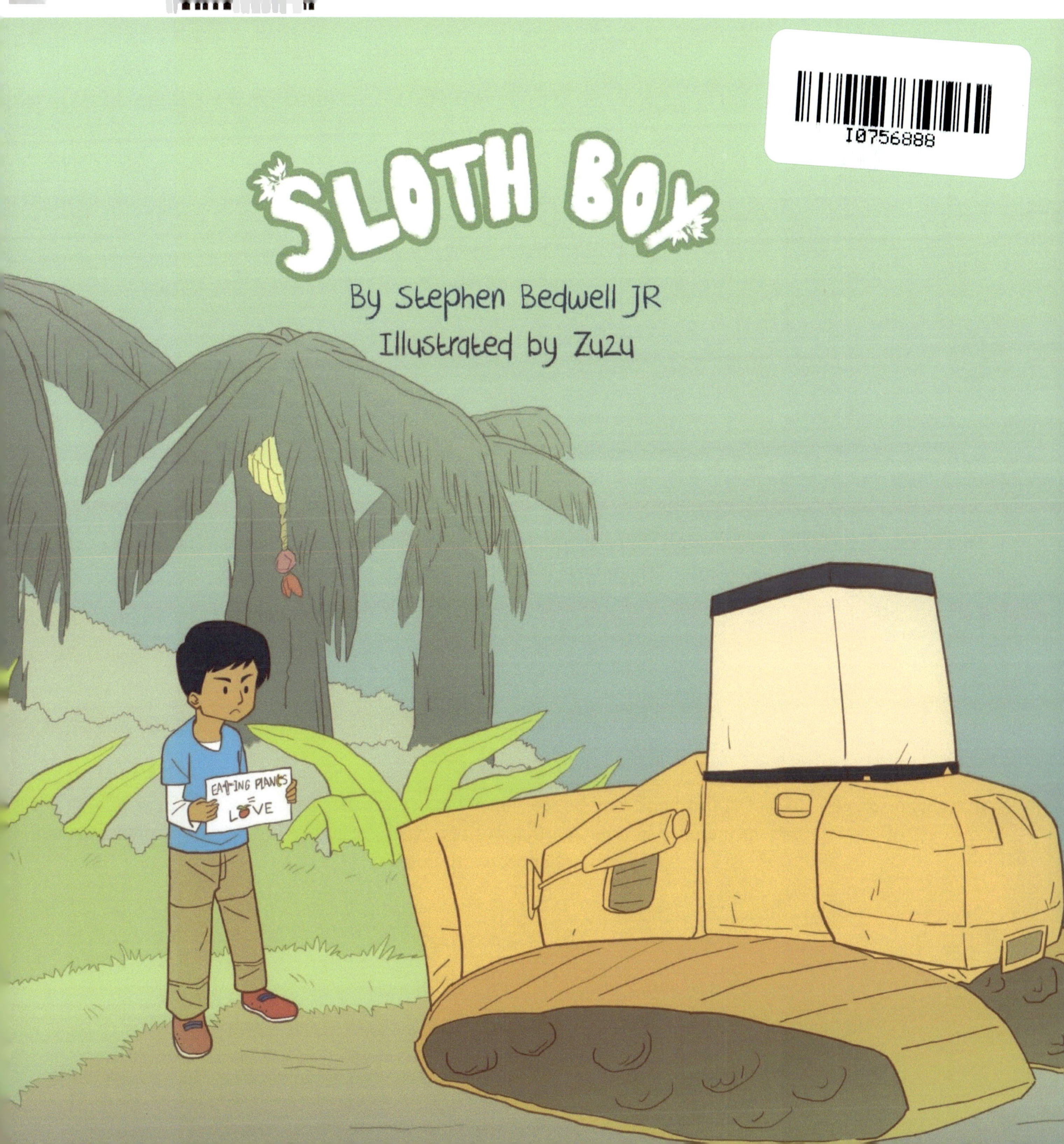

SLOTH BOY
By Stephen Bedwell JR
Illustrated by Zuzu
EATING PLANTS = LOVE

Illustrations by Zuzu

ISBN-10: 1986251829

ISBN-13: 978-1986251822

DEDICATION

To Mom:
You never doubted and always lovingly watered this tree of health and compassion.

The sun shines bright through my window.
Mom yells in, "Get ready to go!"
Leaping to my feet, I hurry on my way.
Throwing on some clothes, I say,
"This will be a great day!"

I cannot believe how lucky I get to be.
I am going on a rainforest vacation with Mommy and Daddy!
Quickly, I race out of my little bedroom nest.
In the kitchen, I eat my morning breakfast.

Traveling with Mom and Dad,
we are on our way.
I will soon be in
a great rainforest later today.
We coast down the hills and
switch between lanes.
Next, I will be flying high on
some planes.

We arrive on the plane and patiently wait to take flight.
Soon we will be flying above at such a great height.
All around the world these planes go.
From places of warmth to places of snow.

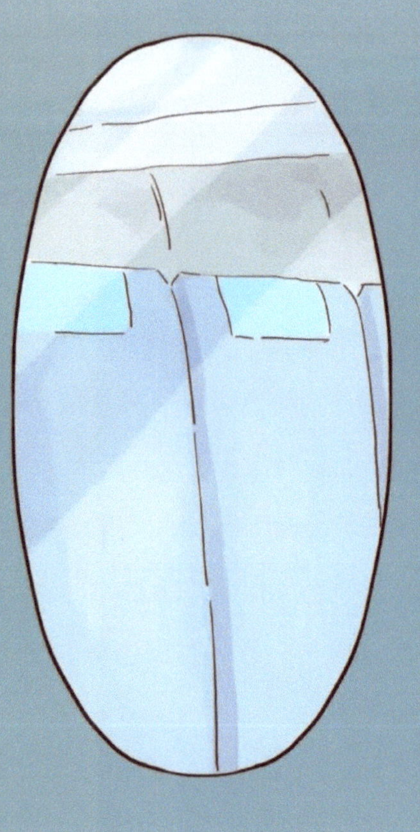

Mom tells me that we are getting close to our destination.
She says, "When you see the rainforest, you will see lots of vegetation.
The rainforest is made up of rivers, streams, bushes, and large treetop canopies.
It is home to millions of beautiful plant and animal species."
AMAZING RAINFOREST

We have landed and touched the ground.
Mom tells me, "Next we are resort-bound!"
We drive quickly along the coast and up through the mountains.
I am so excited! Now our rainforest adventure begins!

Wow! Look at this! This place looks like a giant fort!
Mom laughs and tells me, "This is an eco-resort.
Let's go look around and explore, shall we?"
I throw my hands in the air and yell, "Yippee! Yippee!"

We meet our friendly host and he wants to show us all around.
He says, "Where should we start?" I say, "How about the ground?"
Our host walks with no shoes on the soil, grass, and sand.
He says it is good for his health and connects him to the land.
EATING
PLANTS
= LOVE

Our host tells us that all the food we will need, here it is grown.
I look around at the bushes and trees. Some I have never known.
Look at the bananas, mangoes, coconuts, jackfruit, oranges, and mangosteen.
The papaya, pineapple, dragonfruit, sapodilla, and vanilla bean.

Fruits all over! Fruits all over! I can see them all.
Some are very small and some are as big as a ball.
I pick and try so many colorful fruits. Oh, how great they taste!
Holding the peels, our host says, "Let me show you where to put the waste."

Next to the vegetable gardens are big piles and bins.
This is where I throw the garden scraps and all my fruit skins.
It will eventually break down into healthy soil. It is called compost.
"I will be eating tons of fruit and have many peels to add," I tell our host.

All the water used at the resort comes from the many mountain streams.
It is captured and filtered. Nothing could be more healthy and pure it seems.

The swimming pool stays clean with salt and is heated by the sun.
I want to jump and do a cannonball! It will be so much fun!

This resort brings no harm to the Earth. It is such an amazing place.
Our host shares with me, "It is very important to leave no trace.
Always take care of the beautiful Earth and the many animals.
Fresh fruits and veggies should fill our hungry bellies and bowls."

I look up and see many colorful birds traveling in the sky.
Mom points up and says, "Look at the green parrots flying by!"
Our host tells us that the rainforest is filled with so many unique creatures.
He says, "Listen for monkeys, look closely for sloths,
and see birds with colorful features."

The sun is slowly setting and I am starting to feel tired.
All the sunshine, land, and fresh fruit have me very inspired.
I shall tour around more tomorrow and pick up any yummy fruit that fell.
Our host says, "Goodnight! If you have any wonderful dreams tonight,
please do tell."

While deep in sleep, I hear what sounds like scratching on the window.
I quickly sit up in my cabin bed. What is it? I just do not know.

My heart begins to race as I move toward the window.
I am trying to be strong and brave. I move ever so slow.

I slowly pull back the curtain. What is that I see?
Oh, my gosh! It is a two-toed sloth staring back at me!
I decide to run outside. I have never seen a sloth before.
I dart across the floor and quietly sneak out the door.

The sloth says, "Hello! It is nice to meet you!"
I get startled and walk right into the bamboo.
Wow! The sloth is now talking to me. How can this be?
Sloth says, "This resort is beautiful! Look around and see."

"The resort is peaceful and leaves no harm.
It is one beautiful and loving farm.
It grows a ton of different yummy fruits and vegetables.
It does not cut down all the trees or harm any animals."

Sloth tells me that the rainforest,
where he and many species live, is being badly hurt.
Every day trees and plants are being torn down
and machines scrape away the healthy dirt.
They do this so that large acres of land can be factory-farmed.
That is where animals end up being packed in tight and harmed.

Sloth asks to jump on my back to take a little walk.
He shows me all the trees torn down. I am in shock!
All the amazing trees and plants are no more.
There are no animals or birds above that soar.

Sloth teaches me that the rainforest provides the Earth with so much oxygen.
This, however, does not happen when there are no plants and trees within.
Sloth takes me to a giant waterfall where we jump in and swim.
We laugh and play in the water and swing from a tree limb.

I ask Sloth why the rainforest is being taken away.
Sloth tells me, "People have been led too far astray.
There is no need to farm the animals and have them for food.
Eating them and stealing their milk is very mean and rude."

"To be a healthy person and have a strong rainforest, eat only plants.
Let all the rainforest be happy. Monkeys, raccoons, sloths, birds, bugs, and ants.
Fruits, veggies, grains, nuts and seeds are meant to be your food.
Eating them will put you and the animals in a fantastic mood."

Sloth hops up onto my back and we swiftly head back to the eco-farm.
I tell Sloth that I will always make choices that do the rainforest no harm.
I want the rainforest to be full of life and I want to be healthy.
I thank Sloth for our adventure and tell him he has taught me plenty.

I awake to playful birds chirping and the buzzing of bees.
In the distance, I hear the hollering of the howler monkeys.
I step out onto the cabin deck and look upon the rainforest below.
Healthy food choices I must make. I want the rainforest and me to grow.

About the Author

Stephen Bedwell Jr. is a Certified Holistic Nutrition Practitioner who educates children to eat a healthy whole food plant-based diet and encourages children to be environmentally friendly. He achieves this through creative and poetic stories that plant seeds of compassion in the hearts and minds of children. Stephen loves warm weather, sunshine, fruit, and swimming in waterfalls. He is always sure to find time to visit the rainforest.

Be sure to enjoy Stephen's other great books:

Sunflower Kid
Dolphin Girl
Stan the Plant-eater
Stan the Plant-eater: A Trip to the Garden
Stan the Plant-eater: A Trip to the Fruit Market